SELECTED POEMS

Selected Poems

by Ninette de Valois

Published on behalf of the
Friends of Birmingham Royal Ballet
by Carcanet Press

First published in 1998 on behalf of the
Friends of Birmingham Royal Ballet
by Carcanet Press Limited
4th Floor, Conavon Court
12–16 Blackfriars Street
Manchester M3 5BQ

A CIP catalogue record for this book
is available from the British Library

ISBN 1 85754 375 0 (cased)
ISBN 1 85754 376 9 (paper)

The publisher acknowledges the financial assistance
of the Arts Council of England

Set in 11/13pt Perpetua by XL Publishing Services, Lurley, Tiverton
Printed and bound in Great Britain by SRP Ltd, Exeter

*This collection of poems is dedicated to
Her Royal Highness, The Princess Margaret,
Countess of Snowdon*

Acknowledgements

The publication of Dame Ninette's poems has been made possible by generous donations from Mrs Hansi Johnson, Mrs Joy Skinner and the Friends of Birmingham Royal Ballet.

Proceeds from the sale of this edition will go to the Sadler's Wells Development Appeal.

Contents

Introduction *by Graham Bowles*   ix

I

The Beach of Shells (A memory of childhood)   3
The Buddha (In a Museum Garden)   4
The Contented Ghost   5
"He covets the Earth"   6
First Love   8
Nocturne   9
November 11th   10
Song of the Rush Hour (Underground)   11
The Waters of Lethe (A Myth)   12

II

The Crocus   15
The Cycle   16
Dead Cherry Tree in a London Garden   17
Frost   18
Harbour Swans   19
Hidden Copper Beech in Summer   20
The Hills of Arran   21
The Morning is Not Yet Awake   22
Plea to Autumn   23
River Scene at Twilight   24
The Thaw   25
The Tree (Earth's Pipeline)   26
The Wave   27
Winter River   28

III

"I Love Pubs" (Monologue Overheard)   31
Background Music in a Saloon Bar   32
One's Company   33
"Time, Please"   34

IV

Age   3

Candles   3

Castle Ruins on a Cliff Top   3

Theatre in the Round   4

Concorde   4

Continuity   4

Courage   4

Graveyard on a Hilltop (Seen from a train)   4

Migraine   4

The Thames   4

Poppies   4

Poplars   5

Said the Child...   5

V

Alone   5

Clouds   5

Wit versus Wisdom   5

Sleep   5

Rain   5

Remorse   6

Riverside Scene   6

Change   62

I do not like you, Winter!   6

Relaxation   64

A Voyage   6

Song: A Welcome to Old Age   6

Graveyard on a Hilltop   6

Sonnet: Friendship   68

Introduction

Dame Ninette de Valois was born on the sixth of June 1898 in Ireland, in what was to be a much-loved home, "Baltiboys", in Blessington, County Wicklow. There, in the woods and rich pasture land surrounding the River Liffey, sheltered by the quiet beauty of the Wicklow Hills, she spent the first seven years of her life. The setting for this prelude of childhood was as important to her in her future as an artist as was that of the Lake District to Wordsworth or the Dorset landscape to Hardy. Ireland, its countryside and its people were, and have remained, intrinsic to her whole being.

The rest of her childhood was spent in England, first in Kent and then in London, where the name Wordsworth recurs, this time for a dancing teacher, Mrs Wordsworth, at whose school the first steps were taken towards a career that was to make the name de Valois synonymous with the history of classical ballet in England. Professional life began, as it did for many young dancers in those days, early, with a tour in a company called "The Wonder Children", consisting of members of a theatrical school, the Lila Field Academy; this was in 1913 when Ninette de Valois was fourteen and a half. Within the next ten years she had worked in pantomime, musical comedy, music hall, revue, had been the "*première danseuse*" at the Royal Opera House for the first post-(1914–18) war International Opera Season, and then become a member of the Diaghilev Russian Ballet in Paris.

Another decade and she had started her own private dancing school in London, had met and joined forces with Lilian Baylis, becoming a member of the Vic–Wells organization, had contributed to the opening of the Festival Theatre at Cambridge by choreographing their production of the *Orestia* and been involved in subsequent plays there, including Elizabethan and Restoration comedies. In the mid-twenties she returned home to Dublin and to the Abbey Theatre which by then had become internationally recognized, to work with W.B. Yeats, producing and performing in his *Plays for Dancers*. This period brought about contact with the Dublin world of James Stephens, "AE" (George Russell), Lennox Robinson, John McCormack, as well as members of the Yeats family.

So "from quiet homes and first beginnings" her life moved on "out to undiscovered ends" where, in her own words, "the farthest hills are greenest". From the Vic–Wells the Sadler's Wells Ballet would emerge with a permanent home in Rosebery Avenue and from this the Royal Ballet Company at the Royal Opera House, Covent Garden, achievements parallelled by Lilian Baylis's creation of the Old Vic Theatre in the Waterloo Road which would become the National Theatre on the South Bank.

For Ninette de Valois one of the clear prospects of the green hills had been the founding of a full-time educational school to contain and complement the vocational training of classical ballet. This long-cherished hope was realized in 1947 when the Sadler's Wells School was opened at 45, Colet Gardens in West London; eight years later it was to move its junior department to White Lodge in Richmond Park and, with the granting of a royal charter, to become the Royal Ballet School.

This achievement was matched abroad when, also in 1947, the Turkish Government asked Ninette de Valois to set about the founding of a school on similar lines in their country. This was finally established in Ankara. Tireless in her efforts in Turkey, both with the school and the emerging Turkish National Ballet, she saw to it that the best English teachers and choreographers went out there to contribute to the success of these enterprises, and close links, personal and cultural, have remained with them ever since.

All this bears witness to the many aspects of Dame Ninette's life work, but she has always felt them to be related, as she has understood the theatre arts to be, never in separate rooms but integrated and interdependent, for in that interlocking lies their strength and universality. Her autobiographies modestly reflect this and also show her to be as skilful and entertaining a writer as she was a choreographer.

What was not generally known until recently was that she also wrote poetry; she was more than modest about her ability as a poet and it was not something that she spoke of much, although it was close to her heart. There it would have remained had it not been for the encouragement of her colleague and friend, Peter Wright, later to become Director of the newly-formed Birmingham Royal Ballet. Feeling that her poems should be published he asked me to select and edit them for this purpose.

I was most happy to do so, particularly since I had had the good fortune of knowing Dame Ninette for the thirty-five years of my being a member of the academic staff of the Royal Ballet School. In 1985 the first edition, *The Cycle*, was published. It was arranged in four sections and represents her earlier work. In this new edition a further fourteen poems have been added in a fifth section and these were all written later in her life; there was no intention to date them more specifically.

What was specific, however, was Dame Ninette's wish to associate this second edition with her affectionate gratitude to Peter Wright personally and to the members of Birmingham Royal Ballet as a whole, who are so successfully enlarging the scope while preserving the traditions of the Company she founded.

Graham Bowles
London, 1998

I

The Beach of Shells
(A memory of childhood)

Focused intently now the whole of her eight years...
What magic in the loveliness upturned!
A myriad curved openings, rainbow-hued.
    As sings the sea
    And croons the wind.
A sharp delight is hers as the crackling shells escape
And tumble through her fingers when hard pressed to
Her slender form.

Her child mind does not seek perception,
Blessed as it is to the point of pain,
Yet wildly happy.
The world she knew is blotted out,
There is just herself, fiercely alone,
Alone with God.

If the great beach and its oneness could stay
Forever, and share its thoughts and be her friend,
The sea as well a part of her, forever...

All secrets known and nothing said.

But along the shore she knows a storm will come,
And roughly fall upon the chanting shells...
    One shell she presses to her ear that tells
She may not know such happiness again.

Stilled moment in a heart of innocence.

The Buddha
(In a Museum Garden)

London holds within these walls heaped treasures,
Heirs apparent to unmeasured time.
They hoard rich findings that
Man looks at with incertitude
Making his shuffling round.
Children run and shout; they press
Spread-eagled fingers on glass cases
To make damp transfers.
Light from the long, chaste window draws our gaze
Down to the courtyard, where the spring array
Of a cherry tree has reached its tight-packed zenith.
Near the splashings of the fountain's jet
Are students, seated, sensing that strange peace
Of waters leaping upwards in content.

Hushed in meditation sits the god,
And all is pregnant with arrested thought
As beauty seeks for wisdom in retreat.

The Contented Ghost

If you should see me by the shore
    Just leave me on my own
By tumbling wave, and note no more
    My form of shining tone.
For out of time is all now set,
    Thought enshrined in light;
A deep content is fully met –
    Detachment scales a height.

No more my heart can grief contain
    Since lost is earthly tie,
And memory now feels no pain
    For senses born to die.
So should you feel my presence near,
    Stand still and ponder on
The needless thrust of fearful fear –
    And I will wander on.

"He covets the Earth"

"Russell had just come in from a long walk on the
Two Rock Mountains, very full of his conversa-
tion with an old religious beggar who kept
repeating 'God possesses the heavens, but he
covets the earth – he covets the earth'."

Yeats

* * *

Where the peat is sliced as a sticky brown cake
And steams in the trench of a warm earth that breeds
The greenest of green.
When the hills display their haphazard curves
The wild one declaims his suspicion,
As backed by his shrewd yet panicky mood
He continues to raise his keen...

"He covets the earth, aye, He covets the earth"

As he stalks his way through the time-worn climbs
And the sticky peat sucks at his feet,
Comes fear that the turf of the good, green earth
Hordes food for the Garden of Eden.

They claim him to be a real Holy One,
(In Ireland things go to the head)
As many a mystical caper of mind
Has been thought to be wrought
By the Lord's Little People.

So he cries to the sky as the clouds scurry by
Hustled by worrying winds,

"In the name of the Saints, isn't Heaven enough?"

Yet all he could feel was celestial rebuff,
And all he could say with his foresight at bay:

"He covets the earth, aye, He covets the earth."

First Love

First love seeks no summer peak
Its innocence is evergreen;
Just in the mind a tranquil thought
That senses time has ever been.
It shares the lark's ascending sway
And lives in full the gleaming day;
Claims virgin sight so crisp and clear
And youth's fresh mind that lacks all fear.

First love in its hinterland
Holds the breath of quietness;
Knows the feeling that is spent,
Still bestows its fruitfulness.
A life astir, a bird on wing,
Demand a song on earth to sing;
Though Orpheus may play again
And pluck the strings of buried pain.

Nocturne

"We broke the seal of Coleridge's
letters, and I had light enough to see that
he was not ill. I put it in my pocket. At
the top of White Moss I took it to my
bosom — a safer place for it.

N.B. The moon came out suddenly...
and a star or two beside."

D. Wordsworth

Was the swell of the moon
The heart's dilation
In an upsurge of pain?
    No... It was love's resilience
That created the glow.

Stars, feeling the call,
With charity spilt
Their clarity.

Through the echo of words from a poet's mind,
And light that makes space eternal,
In the glow of the moon and the service of stars
    Painless the progress of sorrow.

November 11th

... It comes, this yesterday,
An incandescent ray...
　　　All hearts transcend.

Fostered love through life
Needs no sharpened knife
　　　To penetrate.

As breath of life feeds thought,
There is true awareness wrought
　　　Without pained thrust.

Remembrance vividly
Lives on, an ecstasy
Alongside their Free Will.

Song of the Rush Hour
(Underground)

I'm a fugitive with this guitar
Watching the rat race run,
Outside that stream of flummery
My quizzing brain is flung.

Globular passage underground
Echoes my bawdy tune,
As this slothful starfish cartwheels
Flaunting its broody gloom.

Splayed out in apathy far down
Is the basement of my mind;
For me there is no sympathy
I'm just a roof untiled.

A drop-out drops out from it all
To pick up some new clue;
These foozled crowds are not for me
        (But then I am so few).

The busy bees are circumspect
Of all things left undone.
Man seems intent to make God's Word
Severe and meddlesome.

Would Christ come down and then come see
The drainpipe life man lives,
Then this guitar would go on air
And broadcast what He bids.

The Waters of Lethe
(A Myth)

We do not remember the soul's long venture
As we drink yet again of the waters of Lethe.
To forget leaves nothing to heed,
      There's no sound...

Thirst is not quenched when we drink of the waters
That deaden the song of the sphere's full voice
And smother the beat of the earth's deep pulse.

Homesick Ones!
We are blinded again with Earth's journey renewed,
For we cannot reclaim
Sight, drowned by the waters of Lethe.

Alone in her love Echo's cry is not heard,
As everyman sees
But his shade in the waters of Lethe.

Pale the narcissus that springs from the bank.

II

The Crocus

With confidence the crocus lifts its head,
The height is measured by the hedging grass
That guards the progress from a trustful birth
To meet the spring's caress.
Cosseting spring!
You have a hold that kills expectancy
And leaves the petals in mute disarray
To fence with potency.
It is the course of youth to ripen or to fade
In servitude to its own summer day...
A seedling born and wholly free
Or seized instead by enmity.
Perennial life is pledged to heed
An unknown force that holds it to
A rhythm rife before
The birth of earth.

The Cycle

The cycle turns to sap and blood...
The seasons' fourfold intercourse
Sets motion in a whirling flood
That would destroy the blossom's bud.
The centre has a Cyclops' sight –
A one-eyed kernel deeply cleft.
      Fire and flame; then limpid night
      On a seeker casts bespoken light.

Life wanders at length in borrowed time...
Behind a mind and eye bewitched,
And would find the rest of an ancient rhyme
Whose echoed lilt has built a shrine.
As a magnet they work in harmony,
When earth and sky conceive through rays
      And thought, midst such fertility,
      Feels birth and death spell unity.

Pale is the legend of life on earth...
An interchange of thought and deed
With halcyon heights at full-drawn breath
And secret findings reached by stealth.
Vibration – spring time's ancient rôle –
Has brief command of the measured way,
      For elements in concord tell
      The one in universal soul.

Dead Cherry Tree in a London Garden

The vertical stretch of the trunk,
With its outward spread,
An umbrella feeling its way...
Once the colourful curve of the frame
Drank the showers of May.

Now twigs that are sapless project
With a blemished thrust.
The outline may still take the name
Of umbrella, but lost is the silk
To cover the frame.

Deflated appear your dead branches,
Yet you pushed through the soil
Filled with a life-giving urge.
Quiescent is total destruction
Through a negative purge.

Cool notes from the throat of a dove
As a shudder enfolds you...
More passive than petulant spring
Is your shrink from the blast of rebirth
And pollution's sharp sting.

Frost

Highlighted seems the work of creation
As, edged with this frigid touch,
Nature conforms with elation

And yields to the skill of delectable strokes
From a magically wrought cosmetic,
Whose brushwork neatly invokes

The spread of the ice, on whose glazed face
A tarpaulin creeps, disguised
As pernickety, wrought point lace

That covers as well the robin's wing,
For nothing escapes an eye
That conjures up patterns to wring

From its crystallized throttle the death cry of love...
Yet forever returns
The leaf of a branch
Once held in the beak of a dove.

Harbour Swans

                                 ... Low Tide:
With sloth you seep and with ebbed waters reap
          A disenchanted scene
Disclosing mud, whose oozy rufflings
Rest on stretches of its linear flow.
A swan accepting compromise has come
With black webbed feet. This slottish splay
Supports the snowball frame that holds
Features soiled with clinging streaks of sludge...
          In search of things asleep
          In tired time, engulfed in débris deep.

                                High Tide...
This gangster of swift buoyancy now shows
          A cobweb thinly spread
On bouncing waters struggling with the light
Whose certitude no rope could bind.
Swan of the lordly neck and princely stretch
Now floats in symmetry upon the water's flux –
          Serpent of Eden purified
                    ... And paradise regained.

Hidden Copper Beech in Summer

Alone I stand. A muted red
Embraces me. Encased
My glow with its overflow
At bay in dark seclusion.

With haste I thrust my branches through
The evergreen nearby.
I choke it in my frenzy
To find a place to grow.

But no. The thrust is ostracized.
And so I wait
For the deep half-tone
Of an autumn day
To frame
My red-brown glow.

The Hills of Arran

It must have been an anguished sea that flung you up
On the summit of its waters. Now we see you flushed
With the heather's glow or the snow's chilled white
That wears a nun's serenity.
The loves you know are the clutch of low-flying clouds
That dip and dab, licking your peaks then leaving you with
The mountaineers that stab, or the black-faced sheep that tear
At your breast with the tug of hungry babes.

Dusk is here, sharpening the outline of these heights.
Dark tones descend to sweep your sides with majesty.
As day fades, there rises from the depths
An alerted stag in silhouette.
The questioning outline of his antlers stands on guard,
Yet these rugged bastions have a beauty bred
From mystery, once conceived in the forestry
Of streamlined trees and sweeping boughs.

Rocks that are loose now somersault and reach the sea.
These outcasts from the hills know the clasp of greedy waters
That sap and circle, etching the land once hurled
As garbage to the elements.
The sea is a libertine, possessive and obsessed,
Indulgence is asked of all for the roughness of its kiss,
As the hills of Arran learn from the shrieking gales
Of sea and air's tough unity.

The Morning is Not Yet Awake

The morning is not yet awake,
The languid stretch of day
Is negative
And filled with sloth.

Bewildered birds skim earth and tree
As a plane descends from the height it reached
In night
To journey's end.

In its heaving sleep the mist now chokes
The waterway that seeks a breeze
To end
The stifling stay.

Hesitant day thins the light,
Reluctant to spread its clarity.
"But you are born!"
Cries out
A cocksure dawn.

Plea to Autumn

Don't fade too soon.
You wear the cast-off clothes of summer with the elegance
Of a woman challenged by the middle years of life.
Serene your ordered colours in their subtle overtones.
You have no fainting fits nor strokes of violence,
Only a change of face and a contour filled with grace.

Don't fade too soon.
Let us watch your loveliness surmount
Air that is chilled, yet not made impotent through frost.
Inflame your glow and see that time is now arrested
For you to stretch your limbs and linger ever longer...
Just hold your breath, defy and frustrate winter.

River Scene at Twilight

Rough-edged ripples ride the waters.
The sunbeams' shattered frames
Are as broken stars that sigh
And gasp in the succulent clasp
Of waters that are alien
To mercy born of love...
Midst the dazzle of their dust
The sunbeams lie
And die,
A twilight In Memoriam to day.

The Thaw

Snow lies abandoned...
Its outline awry.
The lick of the thaw
Makes earth show the swell
Of a pregnancy spring has begun.
In league with the sun
This gluttonous womb
Seeks a sip of the flaccid snow.

Snow lies abandoned...
Servile servants of cycle
Are cracks on the ice
And flickers of frost on the buds.
Rising as periscopes from
The submarine soil that they serve,
Do the tree trunks observe
Their branches have lost their white frills?

Snow lies abandoned...
As winter retreats
In awe of the thaw,
And the cycle of birth
Returns to the earth
Once more.

The Tree
(Earth's Pipeline)

The bark is tattooed with long wrinkled lines,
The trunk a pipeline for rich flowing sap –
By demand of the tree, the sap flows on
To the tip of each branch.
The leaves are her children; abandoned they seem
When lured from the tree by the call of the earth.
As the tree sucks again from the earth and the sky,
A life force is sought once more to replace
The free-loving leaves wrenched from her grasp.

Maternity scales unexplored heights –
Seclusion is sought with a godlike intent,
From where she will sow with tight-lipped content
Life's flow.

The Wave

This symmetry that seeks a proud return
Draws back in froth; soft flowing disarray
Retreats within itself to curve again
In arched control — with fringe of flecking foam.
This beach of shining gold complacent lies
Till breaking wave, with high-flung tears that sting,
Dispels with callous air that calm content...
Scattered on wetted sands the helpless spray
Awaits the call of death from sun and wind
In selfless homage to the wanton wave.

      Within its forceful thrust of rising strength,
      Amidst the hurling of its warrior cry,
      The newly swelling lordliness accepts
      The low intone of an epic, ringing sigh.

Winter River

Bare trees, strange skeletons in silhouette,
Their outlines like an etching faintly wrought,
Cast a shadow on the river's edge
Where jaundiced willows drop discredited,
Whose verdant glory once was summer's pride.
The curtailed day deflates reluctantly
And seagulls' wings reflect two shades of steel
As mirrors catch the winter shafts of light.
How sharp the bite, how bright the icy kiss
Of darting cold; pale stillness reigns
And muted earth succumbs to night's caress.
But dawn reveals the earth wears crystal crowns
That steal brief glory from the rising sun:

Thus beauty meets her fate with shining face.

III

"I Love Pubs"
(Monologue Overheard)

The old one enters and orders her drink...
"I'm alone," she says,
"Here and elsewhere.
But pubs are not lonely and I don't have to think."

"No pushing, no jostling, casual and kind
Is the company here.
You don't have to speak.
I'm lonely you see, but here I don't mind."

"And the music they play is muffled and slow.
An old person's life
Stands still at the end
That's something the tunes seem to know."

"I love pubs; I've always done so.
They are quiet and solid,
There's peace in the mind
With everyone moving just to and fro."

And I do the same...

Background Music in a Saloon Bar

There's no intrusion,
A rocking-chair soothing the mind
Breeds seclusion.

Between slow gulps of red wine
My fingers play on the glass.

A song becomes sad,
There are words now that pluck at the nerves
Of the mind's blotting pad.
Broken jigsaw, your shapes do not tally,
So memory beats a retreat.

There's a sudden intrusion.
The melody's whimsical moan
        Breeds confusion.

Now everyone stirs and makes note of the time,
I'll soon be alone with this glass of red wine...

One's Company

Unfettered seems the isolation...
As he talks in undertones
Jumbled arguments become
Thin waters of a running stream.
Punctuation, articulation,
Skill of the well-turned phrase
Have no place in the flurried flow.
Does he hear the radio play?
An accessory to his journey
Towards that impasse
The years have willed.

There is sympathy around...
From the barside comes a query that bestows
Rough-edged companionship.
       "What price Arsenal
       Next year, mate?"
Attention is now alerted,
Shared by bottles tilted to serve
Their meticulous measure.

The ensuing pause highlights
A dignity in the pitch of his voice:
       "I haven't the slightest idea."
Sentence completed.
There's no more to say.

Here in The Local fraternity greets
Liberty's easeful licence.
His confusion is calmed. He slips once again
Into the cleft deftly cut to protect
His seclusion.

"Time, Please"

Pub with panes of sweating crystal glass,
Swing doors that know their place must now clock in...
Openings and closures moan like tight-hinged sighs.

Pop tunes, by tinkling glass and clanking mug,
And turbulent thoughts the fumes have bred
Are trapped as tape-recordings in the brain.

Salubrious the sway of the liberties of song.
Far-flung words, that hold the tang of seaspray,
Drown in the shouts that somersault in space.

The dartboard stands aloof in expectation, as
The flash of a ribald wink from a juke-box bulb
Hails smoke clouds mating with the stench of beer.

A final gulp of the "Time, Please" chime of time
Sees pavements greet the disarrayed ejection
As quaysides accept the catch of netted sprats...

Pub with the panes of sweating crystal glass,
Swing doors that know their place must now clock out...
Closing the pendulous sway of the big-mouthed gap.

IV

Age

The aged are placed on shelves,
Dim night-lights weeping wax,
Frail biscuit china chipped.

Pills are known to fortify
And help the effort made
To spread thinned peacock tails.

Cut the pills; let life be
More deeply felt, then lived.

Candles

Slim wax candles on
A Christmas tree,
With spearpoint flames
Outstripping
The fir tree's tracery,

Rock the world again
In candlelight
That is the first born
Flame of peace.

It is birth,
This gift of light –
In sombre night
And silent snow.

*

Rebirth bountiful
In annual chestnut-spread,
A flowered peak
Of valiant bloom,

Rose flushed or full white,
This candlelight
With upward reach that says
All life, all death –
Just one.

Castle Ruins on a Cliff Top

The floodlight's warm, square face
Possessively ascends
The sea-sprayed sweating walls
And picks out pock-marked stones.
Sculptured by time and turbulent gale
Such petrified pageantry knows
The chill and the sting of tears
Wrought through the years by sea-borne storms.
Deep in layers of earth
Lie symbols of life –
Skulls with hollows that hold
Secrets of tortured souls.

As night frowns on these empty sands
Waves rise with sighs from the reef of time.

Theatre in the Round

Play without a curtain?
You see, it makes for newness,
And beat rhythm, king of stupor,
Voices an order with accent on monotony.

This shouting with its blank brand of silence
        Creates a vacuum.
Whose effort is it?
Computer minds at work
Intent on novel means of eruption
        To safeguard fear?
            We do not know, and so
It is not possible to understand.

*

Antigone, are you still with us
To prove our brotherhood?
Would you once more defy
A law that suffocates the truth?

To you, Antigone, a law can be
A wreath with its stem tight coiled
And stiffened with fine wire
To hold in subjugation
A truth long buried...

*

Theatre in the round...
You have been here before, when
A star played the rôle of spotlight,
But progress suffered misconception
Through the antics of its unskilled players.

*

Could there be a spiral
Tapered to reach the spotlight star
And share its tranquil light?
No noise that way, no rough awakening,
No tape recorder voicing fallacies

And still no curtain blotting out or fading in.

Concorde

Inverted beauty thrusts...
Taut the wings in their upward soar.
Vibration dies; velocity full stretched
Now unifies speed, space and time.
Intangible is symmetry conceived
In the deeper shades of mind.

No Phoenix will challenge this proud beak.

Continuity

To be abreast
With thrust of time
And heart astir.
Sense golden song
Of yesterday
Will come and go.
Note smooth recoil
Of shadows that
The mind would stay,
Child wonderment,
Youth's surety,
Maturity...

The circle that
Is now complete,
Do I repeat?

Courage

Tense world that would destroy itself,
We are the dramatis personae involved;
Our minds, encased in double-glaze,
Seek the outsized desk, the padded chair
And air-conditioned suite,
To service gilt-edged courage.

Yet courage sometimes travels inwards
Where a vacuum awaits its industry.
There the great barn of the self can face
The fleeting winds of time's contingencies,
Gales of the world that blow in horizontal lines.
Yet they know the power of the draught,
And courage is a draught.

Graveyard on a Hilltop
(Seen from a train)

Silenced the voice of swinging bell,
As church with stately gaze
On you unfolds this night its trust,
    A sentinel of love.

*

You have an air serene, apart
    As sleeping children,
Lovely and unafraid and tired out with play.

*

Austere the tree that guards your sleep,
The matron of your world.
The moon aloft silvers your bed,
Dim night-light of your dreams.

*

You have an air serene, apart
    As sleeping sorrows,
Content and stilled in tranquil timelessness.

Migraine

This pain in the head, so utterly one's own,
Is not the same as in the arm or leg
Which have affinity
With other arms and legs.
But in the head – Oh no!
It is unique, an almost abstract pain
It's so alone.

Dappled fancies; shooting lights; confusion.
There is no way to by-pass
This chaos which so occupies my head,
No outlet for those jostling thoughts that are
Too dead to shape ideas,
Yet too alive for dreams.

Nothing to do. Imprisoned there
The relentless pain circles without purpose
Till, like a wilful child, confused by coloured bricks,
Who topples the bright structure he had built,
My head discards its pictures –
That cubistic array with their painful, sharp edges.

As a balloon deflating with a faint, low sigh
My head becomes aware of weightlessness.
Back comes the urge to fill
This peaceful void with foolishness,
Thoughts heavy with importance, trimmed with fuss.

Good migraine, since you must come again
I would talk with you
And study your reasonings.
But you will wait awhile,
For your return can only be
Through contact with ideas that harass me.

The Thames

            Crumbled history tumbles
To meet the waters, and appease
The hunger of black mud that lies
Glum and covetous.
            The quagmire sucks anew —
            These findings of a tide
That hauls the weakened in its wake.

Great houses line the river banks.
These distant offsprings of a dynasty
Are cherished children, and display
            Self-centred confidence.
Yet stilled the history that frames the present scene, invisible
Are walls surrounding thoughts that once gave birth to deeds.

Only the river sweeps to meet the sea
And there to mingle with oblivion.
For deep and unrelenting proves to be
The levelling of life with shipwrecked loot.

Poppies

It is thought their petals curve
As emblems of death's overflow.
    Does stupor dominate their swerve?

Cold seems their tryst with distant dead
Midst the green of fields in France,
    Where blood was shed of poppy red.

What draws the blaze of poppies from
An earth that knows the knell of strife?
    Springtime, love and birth of life...
These stalwart stems with upward thrust
Show the poppies thrustful course –
    Eternity rejects remorse.

Poplars

The poplars gossip...
Air holds the sound,
The whisperings of
High-borne things.

As harpstrings greet
Fingers that play,
The leaves complete
Their rhapsody.

A quiverful
Of tapered hours
Are motion and sound
At rest above.

*

The poplars gossip...
And the frowning sky
Sees tired day
Fall from its peak.

Said the Child ...

"I love you...
 I shall love you as long as you live
 And when you are dead
 I shall love you as long as I live,
 And when I am dead
 I shall love you as long as God lives."

When death passes by
There is rebirth of love,
Recurring, unswerving,
Philosophically wrought.
        What more can God ask
Of the faithful than this?

Alone

Loneliness? It has no real existence,
Just an indulgence that is sought by man.
Within is everything.
To be alone can be reality,
Divorced from daytime's extroversions.
Tranquil is the search for thoughts that are as shadows.
"Seek and ye shall find..."
Find? Yes. Find knowledge that is hidden from
The earthbound mind.

Clouds

I love your hectic rush across the skies
 Or your sun-tipped blushing
 In its sleepy disarray.
Sometimes you appear as bloated beasts
Or the flow of lapping waters,
 Divorced from all aggression.

Clouds! You are happy just to be
 Custodians of those thoughts
 That earth flings up as mists,
  To seek a change of life.

Wit versus Wisdom

Is wit the wayward child of wisdom?
    The touch is light,
    We like it so.

Fortuity is sensed here and
    Might well economize,
Reduce the size of fostered thoughts.

Could wit be wisdom's shorthand,
Quaintly fashioned to curtail time?
Again it may be likened to
Sharp frost-bites that can deftly halt
The drift of puffed-up snow.

We shall never know that wisdom is wise.
    Yet wit is fit to humanize
And, yet again, make wisdom's thoughts
    Considerably reduced in size.

Sleep

Storm-tossed clouds of dreams ill-spent
Hiding the blast of things to come?

A consciousness of man's free will
At liberty beyond the stars?

A fragment of life afloat on the curve
Of its immortality,
Where swerve the wings and other things
Of mind and its liberty?

The daily awakening deftly breaks
An awareness of another world;
It makes the oneness that was ours
Stretch to accept the daydream's state.

Rain

Rain. Dank outbursts of despair,
Weepings that lick the fledging leaves
With the sting of wayward spray.

Rain. It checks the giddy heights
Of light and its overflow,
Holds energy at bay.

Rain. The outcome of its strife
May drown, or crown anew
Man's view of fortune's way.

* * *

Childhood alone knows the flow
Of tears as a bird-witted whirl,
The outlet of intangible fears
Midst fetters as yet unchained.

Remorse

Remorse? It will be so.
In time, as spaced on earth, it stands
A plain law versed to clarify
Cause and its aftermath.
It is for us to find essential self,
The essence that exists
     In openness within.

Riverside Scene

Girl with the halcyon hair
At random, unkempt as ripe corn
Propelled by the wind.
Yet today it's the sun whose rays lightly prance
And join in her hair's wayward dance.

Boy seizes the river's challenge,
Commanding his headstrong driftway –
A waterboard linked to a sail
That extends its belly to hold
A breeze it ensnares to enfold.

Girl on the riverside parapet rests.
A coiled circle of coral pink
Seems the sweater that covers her form.
Patterns give the illusion of encircling caresses
Under the carefree capers of tumbling tresses.

Boy is possessed with the going
Alone on his buoyant seesaw.
As the waters give birth to ripples
That bounce, heave, cut and swirl
By a tide caught up in the whirl.

* * *

On the river rides youth with impetuous force,
On the bank there is a wayward frustration wrought,
Both born to master the passage of time
And the intangible urge for a pattern in life.
Downstream or upstream these embryos wait
Knowing destiny's tide is their streamlined fate.

Change

Change... an earthquake in the mind of man
Of eternity fresh sown
Has no tempi of its own.
The voice of heaven shows its skill
Guiding the rumbles of the will.

I do not like you, Winter!

I do not like you, winter!
      Are you just a great strip-tease,
With time's distortion now displayed
In shivering twigs that hang
From branches that would mimic snakes?
Stark and firm, though, stand the arrogant trunks
      Unabashed at their children's loss of clothes.

A stoic one could call a trunk,
With its solemn, stalwart thrust that
      Disdains its cloistered root.
Winter! You wander with content,
Believing in fury and in your partnership with time.

I do not like you, winter!
Not even when you are dressed in white
To humanise, with a seduction worthy of a bride.
Yet all the time you court the frost
      To strangle any harmless fluff.

But hidden secrets of the earth and sky
In partnership with spring, patiently conspire against you.
      That time machine we know to work
With accuracy beyond the mind of man.

Is there a simile? One winter star
Dispersed the chill of life for those
Who felt the shine, then as now,
A shine that lights up snow, for those who care.

Relaxation

The strife of life now seems remote
Amidst its own arrest.
The mind may seek out quietness
And thus confront new consciousness.

Just fade away those wisps of mind
That have followed their fate in the hollows of life,
Dead, but ever afloat.
Gather them up, bury them whole,
Within the gloom of night.

A Voyage

There is this river that all must cross
With a life-force tide where flickers time,
To the chant of sphere and the dance of stars.
    Yet it may be just a gentle tow
Through the cosmic rays of the rainbow's glow.

Song

A Welcome to Old Age

Memory is the greatest decoy
Of the eye, the mind and the heart;
It should reflect on things that were sought
And bring to the surface all by-passed thought.

Alive is the seed, just note its power
In the rebirth of many an annual flower;
The air is astir in the leaves of the yew,
So why not assume it is God's way with you?
Do not stray, find the measure of living each day.

Graveyard on a Hilltop
(Chagford, Devon)

These sacrosanct trees are interlocked; white are
The slabs of stone with chiselled words that
Faithfully recall the dead,
Who lie deeply buried in the ground.
Each stone and tree, in the care of things unseen,
Demands that its proud stance through time
Defies both climb and clutch of the ivy's green.

Is there a mind astir pursuing a goal,
In the bluster of this restless day?

Privileged spot! Sleeping thoughts discard reflection.
Death's pattern of deduction is not concerned with strife,
Only the perpetuity of life,
As thought forsakes all earthbound aims.

Sonnet

Friendship

Untrammelled feeling from the day of birth
Seals friendship's attitude of heart and mind;
The love unsought – serenest of all kind –
Breeds state of deep content and artless worth.
As toll of bell that swings with echoed mirth
This rhythm soars, and, with the timeless bind
Of senses dipped in laughter's tranquil find,
Seeks sated end in memory's deep earth.
If snowflakes should their death-bed pattern lose,
Intangible the aim of cosmic plan;
For death would come to image sought by love.
Oh Harmony! Could you but find the muse
To sing of wisdom and the hope that man
May seek for friendship's symbol in the dove.